WRITTEN & PUBLISHED BY

KINDLY NYC L.L.C.

DID YOU EAT?

Published by: KINDLY NYC L.L.C.

ISBN: 9798325914003

Text Design by: KINDLY NYC L.L.C.

Cover Design by: KINDLY NYC L.L.C.

With Heartfelt Gratitude

Writing this book has been a wild ride, full of ups, downs, and plenty of coffee. (Seriously, if any coffee makers, farmers, or manufacturers are reading this, feel free to hook me up with a lifetime supply. This might be my first book, but it's definitely not the last!) It wouldn't have been possible without the incredible people who cheered me on, picked me up, and kept me going. So, here's to you, my tribe of amazing supporters!

To My Family: You guys rock! To my parents, whose relentless "Did you eat?" mantra has been my lifeline. Your endless love and care have always been more than just words—they're the cozy blanket that keeps me warm. Thanks for always feeding my heart and soul (and my stomach, of course). Also, thanks for not disowning me despite my creative career choices.

To My Friends: To my select circle of friends (you know who you are), thank you for being my partners in crime. From shared meals to endless laughter and deep chats, you've been my sanity savers. Your support has been my North Star, guiding me through this adventure with a smile. If I become a famous author, rest assured, you'll get all the credit... and maybe some of the blame.

To My Mentors: To my mentors, who put up with my endless questions and occasional rants. Your wisdom and patience have been the secret ingredients that made this book happen. Without your guidance, this project might still be just a pile of sticky notes and wild ideas. You're the real MVPs for not running away every time I walked into the room with "just one more question."

To the Readers: Hey there, awesome reader! Thanks for picking up this book and diving into these pages. I hope it strikes a chord with you and deepens your appreciation for the simple, powerful question, "Did you eat?" May it bring you warmth, a few chuckles, and hopefully no food poisoning.

To the Countless Others: To everyone else whose paths have crossed mine, your kindness and support, no matter how big or small, have left an unforgettable mark. This book is a reflection of all the wonderful moments and people in my life. You might not get royalties, but you'll always have a special place in my story.

From the top and bottom of my heart, thank you.

In a village quaint and bright,
Lived a chef with great delight.
Every morn, with break of day,
He'd cook his meals, then he'd say

"Did you eat?" his voice so clear,
Echoed far and echoed near.
Neighbors smiled, children played,
In his care, their hearts were laid.

One fine day, a stranger came,
Hungry, tired, seeking fame.
"Teach me, chef, your art so fine,
I long to make my dishes shine."

With a nod and knowing glance,
The chef began the culinary dance.
"First, you learn to truly care,
For food is love, you must declare."

Days turned weeks, the lessons flew,
The stranger learned and friendships grew.
But fame and glory filled his mind,
Leaving care and love behind.

He opened a place, grand and vast,
But love for food, a thing of the past.
"Did you eat?" he'd never ask,
Focused solely on his task.

DID YOU EAT?

Customers came, then soon they went,
For something vital had been spent.
Food was fine, but heart was cold,
A lesson learned, a tale retold.

Back he went, with heavy heart,
To the chef who'd played his part.
"Teach me now, what I have missed,
For love and care, I have dismissed."

The chef then smiled, wise and kind,
"To care for others, open your mind.
The food you make, with love instill,
And hearts you'll nourish, a void you'll fill."

"Did you eat?" he asked anew,
And in that question, wisdom true.
For food with love is more than treat,
It's a bond, a joy, a life complete.

So here's the tale, both light and deep,
A lesson strong for all to keep.
In every meal, in every greet,
Ask with love, "Did you eat?"

Did you eat ?

KINDLY NYC

Introduction: The Universal Question

Overview

Imagine this: you walk into your home after a long day, and the first thing your mother or grandmother asks is, "Did you eat?" It's a question so simple, yet it carries a depth of concern and affection that transcends cultures and languages. This book delves into the profound significance of this seemingly mundane question, exploring how it has become a universal expression of care, love, and connection across the globe.

From the bustling streets of Mumbai to the serene countryside of Italy, the question "Did you eat?" is a testament to the unspoken bonds that hold families and communities together. It's a phrase that embodies the essence of maternal love, a concept that has been cherished and celebrated throughout human history. By understanding the cultural, emotional, and psychological layers embedded in this question, we uncover a rich tapestry of human relationships and social customs.

Objective

The primary objective of this book is to explore the cultural, emotional, and psychological significance of the question "Did you eat?" This simple inquiry is more than just about food; it's about nurturing, protection, and the deep-seated instinct to care for loved ones. Through this exploration, we aim to highlight how this question reflects the diverse ways in which love and concern are expressed around the world.

We will journey through various cultures, examining how this question is asked and answered in different societies. We'll delve into historical contexts, psychological perspectives, and sociological implications, providing a comprehensive understanding of its universal importance. By doing so, we aim to foster a greater appreciation for the subtle yet profound ways in which humans connect and care for one another.

Importance of the Topic

Why focus on such a simple question? Because in its simplicity lies a world of meaning. The question "Did you eat?" is a window into the heart of human relationships. It's a question that mothers and women across the globe use to check on the well-being of their loved ones. It's a way of saying, "I care about you," without uttering those exact words.

In many cultures, food is synonymous with love and care. Preparing a meal for someone is an act of service and devotion. Asking if someone has eaten is a way to ensure their well-being and comfort. It's a small gesture that speaks volumes about the importance of nurturing and sustaining those we care about.

Moreover, this question reflects the cultural nuances of different societies. In some cultures, it's a question asked daily, a routine part of family life. In others, it might be reserved for special occasions or moments of concern. By exploring these differences, we gain insight into the values and priorities of various cultures.

Fun Fact:

In Japan, it's common to greet someone with "Tadaima" (I'm home), to which the traditional response is "Okaeri" (Welcome back). Often, a follow-up question might be "Gohan tabeta?" (Did you eat?), showcasing the integration of food and care into daily rituals.

Structure of the Book

To provide a thorough exploration of the question "Did you eat?" and its significance, the book is organized into several thematic chapters, each focusing on a different aspect of this universal inquiry. Here's a brief outline of what you can expect:

The Historical Context

We'll begin with an exploration of the historical roots of maternal care and the role of food in human societies. We'll look at ancient practices and traditions, tracing the evolution of the question "Did you eat?" over centuries.

Quote: "There is no sincerer love than the love of food." - George Bernard Shaw

Cultural Significance

This chapter will take us on a journey around the world, examining how different cultures ask and interpret this question. We'll explore the importance of food in various societies and how it is intertwined with expressions of love and care.

Quote: "All sorrows are less with bread." - Miguel de Cervantes

Psychological Perspectives

Here, we'll delve into the emotional and psychological implications of the question. We'll look at how it fosters bonding and connection, and what it reveals about the human need for nurturing and security.

Quote: "To a mother, a child is like the beam of moonlight." - Chinese Proverb

Sociological Perspectives

This chapter will examine the societal expectations and gender roles associated with the question "Did you eat?" We'll explore how these roles have shaped the practice of asking about food and what it says about the broader social context.

Quote: "A good cook is like a sorceress who dispenses happiness."
- Elsa Schiaparelli

Linguistic Variations

We'll analyze how this question is phrased in different languages and what these variations reveal about cultural nuances. We'll also look at the subtle differences in meaning and implication across languages.

Quote: "Language is the road map of a culture. It tells you where its people come from and where they are going." - Rita Mae Brown

Literary and Artistic Representations

Literature and art have long depicted the act of asking about food as a symbol of care and concern. We'll explore these representations in poetry, prose, and visual art, highlighting the universal appeal of this theme.

Quote: "Art is the lie that enables us to realize the truth." - Pablo Picasso

Modern-Day Implications

Finally, we'll look at how the question "Did you eat?" is viewed and practiced in modern society. We'll examine the impact of technology and globalization on traditional practices and how they are being adapted to contemporary life.

Fun Fact: In South Korea, it's common to ask "Bap meogeosseoyo?" (Have you eaten rice?) as a way of checking on someone's well-being.

Throughout the book, we'll include fun facts, quotes, and references to make the reading experience engaging and enjoyable for readers of all ages. We'll also feature speeches and poems that capture the essence of this universal question, providing a rich and varied perspective on its significance.

By the end of our journey, we hope to have provided a deeper understanding of the simple yet profound question "Did you eat?" and its enduring importance in human relationships. We invite you to join us in this exploration and discover the many ways in which this question connects us all.

Chapter 1: The Historical Context

Ancient Practices and Traditions

In the annals of history, the act of asking, "Did you eat?" holds more than just a literal significance. It is a question that embodies hospitality, care, and a profound sense of duty. To understand its historical roots, we must travel back to ancient civilizations where food was not merely sustenance but a symbol of connection and community.

In ancient Greece, the practice of hospitality, known as xenia, was held in the highest regard. It was a moral obligation to offer food and shelter to strangers, often before even inquiring about their identity or purpose. This tradition underscores the significance of food as a primary means of expressing care and establishing bonds. The Greek poet Homer, in his epic "The Odyssey," frequently highlighted the sacred duty of hospitality. When Odysseus visits the house of Eumaeus, the swineherd, he is first offered food and drink, reflecting the timeless importance of this practice.

Quote: "Let us drink, for it is drinking that leads to conversations and establishes bonds." - Homer, "The Odyssey"

The Romans, too, placed a high value on the act of sharing food. In Roman society, the concept of convivium (banquet) was central to social and political life. It was not merely an event to satiate hunger but a forum for discussion, bonding, and the reinforcement of social hierarchies. A typical Roman banquet included a wide array of dishes, and the host's ability to provide for his guests was a reflection of his status and virtue. Here, the act of asking "Did you eat?" or ensuring guests were well-fed was intrinsically tied to one's reputation and honor.

Fun Fact: The term "companion" originates from the Latin "com" (together) and "panis" (bread), highlighting the importance of sharing meals in fostering companionship.

Evolution of Maternal Care

As societies evolved, so did the roles and responsibilities of mothers. In many cultures, the preparation and offering of food became a primary means through which mothers expressed their love and care. This practice has deep historical roots and varies widely across different cultures.

In ancient China, the importance of food in familial and social interactions is evident in Confucian teachings. Confucius emphasized the role of proper conduct and filial piety, where ensuring the well-being of family members, especially through food, was a key virtue. This is captured in the traditional Chinese saying: "To a mother, a child is like the beam of moonlight." This saying encapsulates the ethereal and nurturing connection between a mother and her child, with food often being the medium of this connection.

Quote: "Filial piety and brotherly submission—are they not the root of all benevolent actions?" - Confucius

In medieval Europe, the preparation of food was one of the central duties of women, especially mothers. The kitchen was considered the heart of the home, and it was here that mothers not only prepared meals but also imparted lessons of life and morality. The communal nature of medieval European households meant that sharing meals was a time for bonding and instilling values.

Speech Analysis: A famous excerpt from a 14th-century speech by Queen Philippa of Hainault highlights the importance of maternal care and nourishment:

"In the hearth of our homes, where bread is broken and souls are nourished, we find our strength. It is here, in the giving and receiving of sustenance, that we forge bonds that no steel can sever."

Food as a Symbol of Love and Care

The act of asking "Did you eat?" transcends the physical need for food. It is deeply intertwined with expressions of love, care, and emotional support. Across different cultures and epochs, this simple question has been a cornerstone of familial relationships and social customs.

In India, the concept of Annapurna, the goddess of food, symbolizes the life-giving and nurturing aspect of food. In many Indian households, the act of feeding someone is seen as a pious duty. The cultural emphasis on hospitality and care is reflected in daily practices. Mothers often equate the act of feeding their children with spiritual and emotional nourishment, reinforcing the sacred bond between mother and child.

Quote: "In the temple of the home, the kitchen is the altar, and the food is the offering." - Indian Proverb

In the Middle East, hospitality is a deeply rooted tradition, and the act of sharing food is central to social interactions. The Arabic concept of karam (generosity) is often expressed through the sharing of meals. It is customary to offer food to guests and even to strangers, reflecting a culture where the question "Did you eat?" is synonymous with care and generosity.

Fun Fact: In Bedouin culture, it is considered impolite to ask a guest directly if they are hungry. Instead, food is presented as a matter of course, ensuring the guest's needs are met without the need for explicit inquiry.

The Role of Food in Religious and Social Rituals

Food has always played a significant role in religious and social rituals, further emphasizing its importance in human connections. Many religious traditions incorporate the act of feeding as a form of worship and community bonding.

In Christianity, the ritual of the Eucharist, or Holy Communion, symbolizes the sharing of bread and wine as the body and blood of Christ. This act of sharing food is a profound expression of unity and love within the Christian community. The communal aspect of this ritual underscores the importance of food in creating and maintaining spiritual and social bonds.

Quote: "For where two or three are gathered together in my name, there am I in the midst of them." - Matthew 18:20

In Islam, the act of sharing food during Ramadan, especially during Iftar (the breaking of the fast), is a significant aspect of the holy month. Families and communities come together to share meals, reinforcing the values of empathy, charity, and unity. The question "Did you eat?" during this period is not just about physical sustenance but also about spiritual and communal well-being.

Speech Analysis: A notable speech by a community leader during Ramadan captures this essence:

"As we break our fast together, let us remember that the act of sharing food is not just about feeding our bodies, but also about nurturing our souls and strengthening our bonds. Let us ask each other, 'Did you eat?' with the intention of fostering unity and compassion."

The Symbolism of Food in Folklore and Mythology

Food and its related questions often appear in folklore and mythology, symbolizing abundance, care, and the sustenance of life. In many cultures, myths and stories highlight the magical and nurturing qualities of food.

In Scandinavian mythology, the Valkyries would serve food and drink to warriors in Valhalla, symbolizing the care and honor given to those who have fought bravely. This act of serving food to the fallen warriors is a gesture of respect and an assurance of their eternal well-being.

In African folklore, the story of Anansi the Spider often includes themes of food and cunning. Anansi's adventures frequently involve acquiring food through clever means, highlighting the cultural importance of resourcefulness and the sharing of sustenance.

Fun Fact: In many African cultures, the communal sharing of food is a key part of storytelling sessions, reinforcing the bond between the storyteller and the audience.

By tracing the historical and cultural evolution of the question "Did you eat?" we uncover its profound significance in human society.

This question, in its many forms, has always been more than just an inquiry about sustenance; it is a reflection of care, love, and the enduring bonds that hold us together. Through the centuries, this simple question has transcended its literal meaning to become a universal expression of humanity's deepest connections.

Chapter 2: Cultural Significance

Asia: The Heartbeat of Family and Food

India: A Feast of Love and Tradition

In India, the question "Did you eat?" is more than just a concern for physical nourishment; it is a profound expression of love and hospitality. The importance of food in Indian culture is deeply rooted in its history, religion, and social practices. The act of feeding someone is considered sacred, and it is often intertwined with rituals and traditions that emphasize care and community.

In Indian households, mothers are often seen as the guardians of the kitchen, the hearth, and the family's well-being. The kitchen is not just a place where meals are prepared; it is a space where love and care are expressed through the act of cooking. The question "Did you eat?" is frequently asked by mothers and other family members to ensure that everyone is well-fed and cared for. This practice reflects the cultural belief that a well-fed person is a happy and healthy person.

Quote: "The heart of a mother is a deep abyss at the bottom of which you will always find forgiveness." - Honoré de Balzac

Food is also an integral part of Indian festivals and celebrations. During festivals like Diwali, Eid, and Pongal, families come together to prepare elaborate meals and share them with loved ones and neighbors. These feasts are not just about indulging in delicious food; they are about strengthening familial bonds and fostering a sense of community. The act of asking "Did you eat?" during these occasions is a way of extending warmth and generosity.

Fun Fact: In South India, the traditional meal served on a banana leaf during festivals is not just a culinary delight but also a symbol of prosperity and respect for nature.

China: Harmony and Nourishment

In Chinese culture, food is synonymous with harmony, health, and prosperity. The question "Did you eat?" reflects a deep-seated cultural value of ensuring the well-being of loved ones. This question is often asked by family members, friends, and even colleagues, highlighting the communal nature of Chinese society.

Confucian teachings have significantly influenced Chinese views on family and food. Confucius emphasized the importance of filial piety and the role of family in maintaining social harmony. Ensuring that family members are well-fed is seen as a fundamental duty and a way of demonstrating respect and care.

Quote: "To eat is a necessity, but to eat intelligently is an art." - La Rochefoucauld

In China, family meals are a cornerstone of daily life. The concept of Chifan le ma? (Have you eaten?) is not just a casual greeting but a reflection of the importance placed on food and family time. These meals are opportunities for family members to connect, share their experiences, and support each other. The act of sharing food is seen as a way of maintaining balance and harmony within the family.

Fun Fact: The Chinese New Year is celebrated with a lavish meal called the Reunion Dinner, where families gather to enjoy symbolic dishes that represent luck, wealth, and happiness.

Middle East: The Generosity of the Table

In the Middle East, hospitality and generosity are deeply ingrained cultural values. The act of offering food is a significant part of social interactions, and the question "Did you eat?" is a common expression of care and hospitality. This tradition is reflected in the concept of karam, which means generosity and is often demonstrated through the sharing of food.

Arab culture places a high value on hospitality, and it is customary to offer food to guests as a gesture of respect and kindness. This practice is rooted in the Bedouin tradition of welcoming travelers and ensuring their well-being. The question "Did you eat?" is not just about providing sustenance; it is about extending warmth and building relationships.

Quote: "He who has bread has many problems; he who has no bread has only one." - Middle Eastern Proverb

In many Middle Eastern households, meals are communal events where family and friends gather to share food and stories. The preparation and sharing of food are seen as acts of love and care. During the holy month of Ramadan, the significance of food and communal eating is especially pronounced. The fast is broken with the Iftar meal, which is often shared with family, friends, and even strangers, reinforcing the values of generosity and community.

Speech Analysis: A speech by a community leader during Ramadan captures the essence of this practice:

"As we gather to break our fast, let us remember that the act of sharing food is a reflection of our faith and our commitment to each other. When we ask, 'Did you eat?' we are not just inquiring about physical hunger, but we are also expressing our desire to nourish each other's spirits and strengthen our bonds."

Fun Fact: In Lebanon, it is common to offer a variety of small dishes called mezze before the main meal. This tradition highlights the importance of sharing and enjoying a variety of flavors together.

Western Countries: Diverse Traditions and Common Bonds

Europe: A Symphony of Flavors and Traditions

Europe is a continent of diverse cultures, each with its own unique culinary traditions. Despite these differences, the question "Did you eat?" is a common thread that runs through many European societies, reflecting care and hospitality.

In Italy, food is central to family life and social gatherings. The Italian phrase Hai mangiato? (Have you eaten?) is often used to express concern for someone's well-being. Italian mothers and grandmothers are famous for their devotion to cooking and feeding their families. Meals are seen as an opportunity to bond, share stories, and create lasting memories.

Quote: "The trouble with eating Italian food is that five or six days later you're hungry again." - George Miller

In France, the art of dining is celebrated, and meals are an essential part of daily life. The French expression As-tu mangé? (Did you eat?) reflects a culture that values good food and good company.

French meals are often leisurely affairs, where the emphasis is on enjoying the flavors and the company. The question "Did you eat?" is a way of showing care and ensuring that loved ones are enjoying the pleasures of the table.

Fun Fact: In Spain, the tradition of tapas involves sharing small plates of food with friends and family. This practice emphasizes the social aspect of eating and the joy of sharing a variety of dishes.

The Americas: A Blend of Cultures and Cuisines

In the United States and Canada, the question "Did you eat?" is often used to express concern and hospitality. In many families, meals are a time to come together and connect. The tradition of Sunday dinner is a common practice where families gather to share a meal and catch up on each other's lives.

Quote: "We must have a pie. Stress cannot exist in the presence of a pie." - David Mamet

In Latin American countries, food is a central part of cultural identity and social interactions. In Mexico, the question ¿Ya comiste? (Have you eaten?) is a common way of expressing care. Mexican cuisine is known for its rich flavors and communal nature. Meals are often shared with family and friends, and the act of offering food is a gesture of hospitality and love.

Fun Fact: In Brazil, the tradition of feijoada, a hearty bean stew, is often enjoyed with family and friends. This dish is a symbol of Brazilian hospitality and the joy of sharing a meal together.

Africa: The Communal Spirit of Eating

In many African cultures, the act of sharing food is a vital part of social life. The question "Did you eat?" reflects a deep sense of community and mutual support. In countries like Nigeria, Ghana, and Kenya, meals are often communal events where family and neighbors gather to share food and stories.

In West African cultures, the tradition of communal eating, where everyone eats from a shared bowl, is a symbol of unity and equality. The act of sharing food is seen as a way of reinforcing social bonds and ensuring that everyone is cared for. The question "Did you eat?" is a way of checking in on the well-being of others and maintaining a sense of community.

Quote: "If you want to go fast, go alone. If you want to go far, go together." - African Proverb

In Ethiopia, the traditional meal injera is often shared with family and friends. The act of breaking off pieces of injera and sharing it with others is a symbol of friendship and respect. The question "Did you eat?" in this context is not just about physical nourishment but also about fostering relationships and showing care.

Fun Fact: In many African cultures, the eldest member of the family is often served first, highlighting the importance of respect and hierarchy in communal eating.

By exploring the cultural significance of the question "Did you eat?" across different regions, we gain a deeper understanding of how this simple inquiry reflects the values and priorities of various societies. Whether it is through the rich traditions of Indian festivals, the harmonious family meals of China, the generous hospitality of the Middle East, the diverse culinary practices of Europe and the Americas, or the communal spirit of African eating, the question "Did you eat?" is a universal expression of care and connection that transcends cultural boundaries.

Chapter 3: Psychological Perspectives

Emotional Implications

The question "Did you eat?" goes beyond mere words; it resonates deeply with emotional undertones that reflect care, love, and concern. From a psychological perspective, this simple inquiry can serve as a powerful tool in nurturing relationships and fostering emotional bonds.

At its core, asking someone if they have eaten is a way to express concern for their well-being. This question often serves as a proxy for saying, "I care about you," or "I am thinking of you." The act of ensuring someone has eaten is intertwined with the basic human need for nurturing and security. Abraham Maslow's hierarchy of needs places physiological needs at its base, indicating that food is a fundamental requirement for survival. By asking "Did you eat?" we acknowledge and address this essential need, laying the groundwork for higher-order emotional and psychological well-being.

Quote: "There is no love sincerer than the love of food." - George Bernard Shaw

In many families, this question is a cornerstone of daily interactions. It reflects an ongoing commitment to caring for one another and maintaining the well-being of family members. When a mother asks her child if they have eaten, it is not just about the physical act of consuming food; it is about ensuring that the child feels loved, cared for, and secure.

Mother-Child Bonding

The bond between a mother and her child is one of the most profound relationships in human experience. Food plays a critical role in this bond, serving as a medium through which love and care are expressed. From infancy, feeding is one of the primary ways mothers nurture their children. This act of feeding is not only about providing nutrition but also about creating a sense of safety and trust.

Psychological studies have shown that the act of feeding can strengthen the emotional connection between a mother and her child. The consistent presence of a caregiver during feeding times helps to build a secure attachment, which is crucial for the child's emotional development. This attachment is further reinforced by the repeated act of asking "Did you eat?" throughout the child's life, serving as a constant reminder of the mother's care and concern.

Quote: "To a mother, a child is like the beam of moonlight." - Chinese Proverb

Research: A study published in the journal Developmental Psychology found that children who experienced regular, attentive feeding interactions with their mothers were more likely to develop secure attachments. These children showed higher levels of emotional regulation and social competence as they grew older, highlighting the long-term impact of nurturing behaviors like asking "Did you eat?"

Psychological Comfort and Stress Relief

In times of stress or emotional turmoil, the question "Did you eat?" can provide comfort and reassurance. Food has long been associated with emotional comfort, and the act of eating can help alleviate feelings of anxiety and distress. When someone asks if you have eaten, it can serve as a reminder to take care of yourself, offering a moment of solace and grounding.

Speech Analysis: A speech by a renowned psychologist emphasizes the comforting role of food in times of stress:

"In moments of emotional upheaval, the simple act of eating can offer a sense of normalcy and comfort. When someone asks, 'Did you eat?' they are not just inquiring about your physical state; they are offering a lifeline, a moment of connection that can help anchor you in times of turmoil."

Quote: "Food is symbolic of love when words are inadequate." -
Alan D. Wolfelt

The Role of Food in Healing and Recovery

Food also plays a critical role in the process of healing and recovery,
both physically and emotionally. In many cultures, special foods
are prepared for those who are ill or recovering from an illness,
reflecting the belief that proper nourishment is essential for healing.
The question "Did you eat?" takes on added significance in these
contexts, serving as a way to monitor and support the recovery
process.

Case Study: In traditional Chinese medicine, the concept of food as
medicine is deeply ingrained. Specific foods are believed to have
healing properties, and meals are often prepared with ingredients that
promote health and recovery. When a family member is recovering
from illness, asking "Did you eat?" is a way of ensuring they are
receiving the necessary nutrients to aid their healing.

Quote: "Let food be thy medicine and medicine be thy food." -
Hippocrates

Food, Memory, and Emotional Connections

Food is closely linked to memory and emotion. Certain foods can evoke strong memories and feelings, transporting us back to specific moments in our lives. The question "Did you eat?" can trigger these associations, bringing to mind cherished memories of family meals, holidays, and special occasions.

Research: A study published in the journal Appetite explored the relationship between food and memory. The researchers found that specific foods are often linked to autobiographical memories, particularly those associated with family and childhood. These food-related memories are usually rich in emotional detail and contribute to a sense of identity and belonging.

Fun Fact: The smell of freshly baked bread has been shown to evoke feelings of comfort and nostalgia for many people, often associated with happy memories of home and family.

Quote: "The smell of good bread baking, like the sound of lightly flowing water, is indescribable in its evocation of innocence and delight." - M.F.K. Fisher

The Psychological Impact of Shared Meals

Shared meals play a significant role in building and maintaining relationships. The act of eating together fosters a sense of community and belonging, creating opportunities for meaningful interactions and conversations. When we ask "Did you eat?" it often leads to shared meals, further strengthening our connections with others.

Speech Analysis: A speech by a cultural anthropologist highlights the importance of shared meals:

"Eating together is one of the most fundamental ways we connect with others. It is a ritual that transcends cultural boundaries and brings people together. When we ask, 'Did you eat?' we are not just inquiring about sustenance; we are inviting others to share in the experience of togetherness and community."

Quote: "The shared meal elevates eating from a mechanical process of fueling the body to a ritual of family and community, from the mere animal biology to an act of culture." - Michael Pollan

Fun Fact: Research has shown that families who eat together regularly are more likely to have children who perform better academically and have higher self-esteem.

Conclusion: The Power of a Simple Question

The question "Did you eat?" is a powerful expression of care and connection that resonates deeply with our emotional and psychological needs. It reflects our innate desire to nurture and be nurtured, to care for others and be cared for in return. Through this simple inquiry, we communicate our love, concern, and commitment to the well-being of those around us.

By understanding the psychological perspectives behind this question, we gain insight into the profound impact it has on our relationships and emotional health. Whether it is through strengthening the mother-child bond, providing comfort in times of stress, supporting healing and recovery, evoking cherished memories, or fostering community through shared meals, the question "Did you eat?" is a testament to the enduring power of human connection.

As we continue our exploration of this universal question, we will delve into the societal expectations and gender roles that shape the practice of asking about food, as well as the linguistic variations that reveal the cultural nuances of this timeless inquiry. Join us in the next chapter as we uncover the sociological perspectives behind the question "Did you eat?" and its significance in different societies around the world.

Chapter 4: Sociological Perspectives

Societal Expectations and Gender Roles

The question "Did you eat?" often reflects deeply ingrained societal expectations and gender roles. Historically, the responsibility of ensuring the well-being of family members, particularly through food, has predominantly fallen on women. This chapter critically examines these gender roles, the inequalities they perpetuate, and the cultural significance of food in this context.

The Historical Context of Gender Roles

Throughout history, women have been seen as the primary caregivers and nurturers within families. This role has been reinforced by cultural, religious, and societal norms, which have often placed the burden of domestic responsibilities, including cooking and feeding, on women. Men, on the other hand, have traditionally been expected to be the providers, focusing on external work and financial support.

Quote: "A woman's place is in the kitchen." - Traditional Saying

While this saying may seem outdated and even offensive by modern standards, it highlights the longstanding association of women with domestic duties. The question "Did you eat?" is emblematic of these gender roles, as it often comes from women who take on the responsibility of ensuring that family members are well-fed.

Gender Inequalities in Domestic Labor

Despite significant advancements in gender equality, women continue to bear a disproportionate share of domestic labor, including cooking and feeding. This imbalance is evident in households around the world, where women spend more time on unpaid domestic work compared to men.

Research: According to a report by the United Nations, women perform three times more unpaid care work than men globally. This disparity extends to cooking and feeding responsibilities, which are often viewed as women's work.

Quote: "Equality is not a concept. It's not something we should be striving for. It's a necessity." - Joss Whedon

The persistence of these gender roles perpetuates inequalities, limiting women's opportunities for education, career advancement, and personal growth. The question "Did you eat?" thus becomes a symbol of both care and the gendered expectations that continue to shape women's lives.

The Role of Food in Reinforcing Gender Roles

Food plays a significant role in reinforcing traditional gender roles. In many cultures, the preparation and provision of food are seen as acts of love and duty performed by women. This expectation is deeply embedded in societal norms, where a woman's worth is often measured by her ability to care for her family through cooking and feeding.

Case Study: In many rural Indian households, girls are taught from a young age to cook and manage household duties. The expectation is that they will grow up to be good wives and mothers, capable of providing for their families through their culinary skills. The question "Did you eat?" becomes a lifelong refrain, reflecting their role as caregivers.

Quote: "The hand that stirs the pot rules the world." - Proverb

Empathy: A Woman's First Nature

Empathy, the ability to understand and share the feelings of others, is often seen as a fundamental aspect of femininity. Women are socialized to be nurturing and empathetic, qualities that are essential for caregiving roles. The question "Did you eat?" is an expression of this empathy, as it demonstrates a concern for the well-being of others.

Research: Studies in psychology suggest that women, on average, score higher on measures of empathy compared to men. This difference is often attributed to both biological factors and socialization processes that encourage women to be more attuned to the needs of others.

Speech Analysis: A speech by a prominent psychologist highlights the empathetic nature of women:

"Empathy is not just a trait; it is a skill that women cultivate throughout their lives. From a young age, girls are encouraged to care for others, to understand their feelings, and to offer support. This nurturing nature is reflected in the simple yet profound question, 'Did you eat?' which embodies a deep concern for the well-being of others."

Quote: "Women are the real architects of society." - Harriet Beecher Stowe

Food and Men's Secondary Nature of Empathy

While empathy is often seen as a woman's first nature, it is not exclusive to women. Men are equally capable of empathy, but societal norms and expectations have historically placed less emphasis on nurturing behaviors in men. However, this is changing as gender roles evolve and men take on more active roles in caregiving.

Case Study: In many modern families, men are increasingly involved in cooking and caring for their families. Fathers who prepare meals and ask their children "Did you eat?" are challenging traditional gender roles and demonstrating that empathy and nurturing are not solely the domain of women.

Quote: "To be a father requires patience, love, and giving up the 'all about me' attitude." - Catherine Pulsifer

The Shifting Dynamics of Gender Roles

As societal norms shift towards greater gender equality, the roles of men and women in caregiving and domestic duties are evolving. The question "Did you eat?" is becoming a shared responsibility, reflecting a more balanced approach to family care.

Research: A study published in the "Journal of Marriage and Family" found that men are taking on more domestic responsibilities, including cooking and feeding, than ever before. This shift is contributing to more equitable partnerships and a redistribution of caregiving duties.

Quote: "The strongest families are those where both partners share the responsibilities and joys of caregiving." - Unknown

Fun Fact: In Sweden, government policies promoting parental leave for fathers have significantly increased the involvement of men in caregiving roles. Swedish fathers are now more likely to take an active role in feeding and caring for their children.

Conclusion: Toward a More Equitable Future

The question "Did you eat?" serves as a lens through which we can examine the complex interplay of gender roles, societal expectations, and the cultural significance of food. While traditionally associated with women's roles as caregivers, this question also highlights the evolving dynamics of gender and the potential for greater equality.

By critically analyzing the gender roles and inequalities inherent in the practice of asking "Did you eat?" we gain a deeper understanding of the cultural and societal forces that shape our lives. As we move towards a more equitable future, it is essential to recognize and challenge these norms, ensuring that empathy and caregiving are valued and shared by all, regardless of gender.

In the next chapter, we will explore the linguistic variations of the question "Did you eat?" and uncover the cultural nuances embedded in this timeless inquiry. Join us as we delve into the rich tapestry of language and meaning that surrounds this universal expression of care and connection.

Chapter 5: Linguistic Variations

Language and Expression

The question "Did you eat?" may seem simple, but its phrasing varies significantly across cultures and languages. These variations not only reflect linguistic differences but also provide insights into cultural nuances and social practices. In this chapter, we will explore how this question is asked in different languages and what these variations reveal about the societies that use them.

Phrasing Across Languages

Language is a powerful tool that shapes our perception of the world. The way a question is phrased can carry different connotations and cultural implications. Let's examine how "Did you eat?" is expressed in various languages and the cultural significance behind these expressions.

Chinese: (Nǐ chīle ma?)

In Chinese culture, the question (Nǐ chīle ma?) is a common greeting that goes beyond its literal meaning. It is often used to show concern for someone's well-being and to express a sense of community and care. This greeting reflects the importance of food in Chinese culture and the value placed on ensuring that others are well-fed and healthy.

Quote: "Eating is not merely a material pleasure. Eating well gives a spectacular joy to life and contributes immensely to goodwill and happy companionship." - Elsa Schiaparelli

Japanese: (Gohan o tabemashita ka?)

In Japanese, (Gohan o tabemashita ka?) literally means "Have you eaten rice?" Rice is a staple in Japanese cuisine and symbolizes nourishment and comfort. This question is often used to check on someone's well-being and to offer hospitality. It underscores the cultural significance of rice and communal eating in Japan.

Fun Fact: In Japan, it is customary to say "Itadakimasu" before eating, which means "I humbly receive." This expression of gratitude highlights the cultural importance of food and the communal experience of eating.

Spanish: ¿Has comido?

In Spanish-speaking countries, the question "¿Has comido?" is a way to show care and concern for someone's well-being. Food is an integral part of social life in these cultures, and sharing meals is a common way to build and maintain relationships. Asking "¿Has comido?" is a gesture of hospitality and a way to ensure that loved ones are taken care of.

Quote: "The secret of success in life is to eat what you like and let the food fight it out inside." - Mark Twain

French: As-tu mangé?

In French, "As-tu mangé?" is a straightforward question that reflects the importance of food in French culture. France is known for its culinary traditions, and meals are often seen as a time for family and friends to come together. This question is a way to express concern and to invite others to share in the pleasure of good food and company.

Fun Fact: The French often use the phrase "Bon appétit" before eating, which translates to "Enjoy your meal." This phrase underscores the cultural value placed on savoring and appreciating food.

Nuances in Meaning

While the literal translation of "Did you eat?" may be similar across languages, the nuances in meaning and context can vary widely. These differences provide valuable insights into cultural attitudes towards food and social interactions.

Korean: (Bap meogeosseoyo?)

In Korean, (Bap meogeosseoyo?) translates to "Have you eaten rice?" Similar to Japanese culture, rice is a fundamental part of Korean cuisine and symbolizes nourishment and care. This question is often used as a casual greeting among friends and family, reflecting a deep-seated concern for each other's well-being.

Quote: "Rice is a beautiful food. It is a very beautiful, simple and nutritious food." - Alice Waters

Italian: Hai mangiato?

In Italian, "Hai mangiato?" is a common way to ask if someone has eaten. Italian culture places a high value on food, family, and hospitality. Meals are seen as an opportunity to come together, share stories, and strengthen bonds. This question is a way to

ensure that loved ones are cared for and to express the warmth
of Italian hospitality.

Fun Fact: In Italy, it is customary to enjoy long, leisurely meals
known as "la dolce vita," which means "the sweet life." These meals
emphasize the joy of eating and spending time with loved ones.

Arabic: (Hal akalta?)

In Arabic, (Hal akalta?) is a way to ask if someone has eaten. This
question is often used to show hospitality and concern for others.
In many Arabic-speaking cultures, sharing food is an important
part of social life, and the act of offering food is seen as a gesture
of generosity and kindness.

Quote: "Food is the most primitive form of comfort." - Sheila Graham

Cultural Implications

The way the question "Did you eat?" is asked and interpreted can
reveal a great deal about cultural values and social norms. These
linguistic variations highlight the importance of food as a means
of expressing care, building relationships, and maintaining social
harmony.

Brazilian Portuguese: Você já comeu?

In Brazil, "Você já comeu?" is a way to ask if someone has eaten. Brazilian culture is known for its vibrant and diverse cuisine, and sharing meals is a central part of social interactions. This question reflects the cultural emphasis on hospitality and the joy of coming together to enjoy good food.

Fun Fact: In Brazil, it is common to share a traditional dish called "feijoada," a hearty black bean stew with various meats, during social gatherings. This dish symbolizes the warmth and hospitality of Brazilian culture.

Russian: (Ty yel?)

In Russian, (Ty yel?) is a way to ask if someone has eaten. In Russian culture, food is an important part of family life and social interactions. Meals are often hearty and communal, and asking if someone has eaten is a way to show care and concern for their well-being.

Quote: "The belly rules the mind." - Spanish Proverb

The Power of Language

Language shapes our experiences and perceptions, and the way we ask and answer the question "Did you eat?" is no exception. These linguistic variations offer a glimpse into the rich tapestry of human culture and the universal importance of food as a means of connecting and caring for one another.

By examining the different ways this question is phrased and understood around the world, we gain a deeper appreciation for the cultural nuances that influence our interactions and relationships. Whether it is through the communal meals of Asian cultures, the leisurely dining traditions of Europe, or the generous hospitality of the Middle East, the question "Did you eat?" transcends linguistic boundaries to express a shared human experience.

In the next chapter, we will explore how literature and art depict the act of asking about food as a symbol of care and concern. Join us as we delve into the rich representations of this universal theme in poetry, prose, and visual art.

Chapter 6: Literary and Artistic Representations

Introduction

The question "Did you eat?" transcends its literal meaning, becoming a profound symbol in literature and art. Throughout history, writers, poets, and artists have used food and the act of asking about it to explore themes of love, care, community, and identity. This chapter delves into the literary and artistic representations of "Did you eat?" and examines how this simple question has been depicted and interpreted across different cultures and eras.

Quote: "Art is the lie that enables us to realize the truth." - Pablo Picasso

Food in Poetry: Nourishing the Soul

Poetry has long been a medium through which the complexities of human emotions are expressed. The act of sharing food and the question "Did you eat?" often serve as metaphors for deeper connections and care.

Example: In Pablo Neruda's poem "Ode to the Tomato," the simple act of preparing and eating food becomes a celebration of life and unity. The tomato, a humble fruit, is transformed into a symbol of communal sharing and nourishment.

Quote: "The street filled with tomatoes, midday, summer, light is halved like a tomato, its juice runs through the streets." - Pablo Neruda

Analysis: Neruda's vivid imagery and personification of the tomato illustrate the joy and abundance that come with sharing food. The communal aspect of eating is highlighted, reflecting the cultural significance of food as a means of bringing people together.

Fun Fact: The tomato, once feared as a poisonous fruit in Europe, is now a staple in many cuisines worldwide, symbolizing how cultural perceptions of food can change over time.

Prose: Stories of Sustenance and Connection

In prose, the act of asking "Did you eat?" often serves as a pivotal moment that reveals character relationships and societal values. From novels to short stories, food is a recurring motif that signifies care and connection.

Example: In Laura Esquivel's novel "Like Water for Chocolate," food plays a central role in the narrative. The protagonist, Tita, expresses her emotions and communicates with her family through the meals she prepares. The question "Did you eat?" becomes a way for characters to connect and understand each other on a deeper level.

Quote: "The joy of living was wrapped up in the tortilla. It didn't matter if she was alone; she had food, and that was enough." - Laura Esquivel, "Like Water for Chocolate"

Analysis: Esquivel's novel highlights the power of food as a form of expression and communication. Tita's cooking becomes a language of its own, conveying her love, pain, and desires. The question "Did you eat?" is a thread that ties the characters together, emphasizing the importance of food in their lives.

Fun Fact: "Like Water for Chocolate" is not only a novel but also a cookbook, with each chapter beginning with a traditional Mexican recipe, further blurring the lines between food and storytelling.

Visual Art: The Canvas of Care

In visual art, food and the act of eating are depicted in ways that reveal cultural practices, societal norms, and emotional connections. Artists use food as a symbol to explore themes of abundance, community, and care.

Example: In Norman Rockwell's painting "Freedom from Want," a family gathers around a table for Thanksgiving dinner. The central figure, the grandmother, presents a large turkey, symbolizing the care and effort put into preparing the meal.

Quote: "The centerpiece of the painting is not the turkey, but the act of giving and sharing." - Art Critic

Analysis: Rockwell's painting captures the essence of familial love and care. The question "Did you eat?" is implicit in the scene, as the family members' smiles and anticipation reflect their gratitude and appreciation for the meal and for each other. The painting serves as a timeless reminder of the importance of communal meals in fostering relationships.

Fun Fact: "Freedom from Want" is one of Rockwell's "Four Freedoms" paintings, inspired by President Franklin D. Roosevelt's 1941 State of the Union address, which outlined four fundamental freedoms everyone should enjoy.

Theatre and Film: The Drama of Dining

Theatre and film often use food and dining scenes to develop characters and advance the plot. The act of asking "Did you eat?" can reveal underlying tensions, unspoken emotions, and the dynamics of relationships.

Example: In the film "Eat Drink Man Woman," directed by Ang Lee, the story revolves around a Taiwanese family and their complex relationships, expressed through elaborate Sunday dinners prepared by the father, a master chef.

Quote: "The kitchen is a battlefield. It's not just about food; it's about life." - Ang Lee

Analysis: The film uses food as a metaphor for communication and conflict resolution. The father's meticulous preparation of meals is his way of caring for his daughters, even as they navigate their own personal struggles. The question "Did you eat?" is central to the film's exploration of family dynamics and cultural identity.

Fun Fact: "Eat Drink Man Woman" was nominated for the Academy Award for Best Foreign Language Film in 1994, highlighting its universal appeal and the power of food as a storytelling device.

Music and Song: The Melody of Meals

Even in music, the act of sharing food and the question "Did you eat?" find expression. Songs often use food-related imagery to convey emotions and tell stories.

Example: In Harry Chapin's song "Cat's in the Cradle," the recurring mention of meals symbolizes the passage of time and the evolving relationship between a father and son.

Quote: "When you're coming home, Dad? I don't know when, but we'll get together then. You know we'll have a good time then." - Harry Chapin, "Cat's in the Cradle"

Analysis: The song uses the act of sharing meals as a metaphor for missed opportunities and the longing for connection. The question "Did you eat?" is implied in the son's desire to spend time with his father, highlighting the emotional weight of shared meals in nurturing relationships.

Fun Fact: "Cat's in the Cradle" became a number-one hit in the U.S. and remains a poignant reminder of the importance of family time and connection.

Modern Interpretations: Food in Digital Media

In the digital age, food continues to be a significant theme in various forms of media, from blogs to social media platforms. The question "Did you eat?" is often used to engage audiences and foster a sense of community.

Example: Food bloggers and vloggers frequently use the question "Did you eat?" to connect with their followers, sharing recipes, cooking tips, and personal stories.

Quote: "Food is the ingredient that binds us together." - Unknown

Analysis: In digital media, the question "Did you eat?" serves as a way to build virtual communities and share cultural practices. Food bloggers create content that resonates with their audience, using food as a common thread to connect with people from diverse backgrounds.

Fun Fact: The hashtag #foodporn has over 250 million posts on Instagram, showcasing the global fascination with food and its visual appeal.

Conclusion: The Art of Asking "Did You Eat?"

The question "Did you eat?" is more than a simple inquiry; it is a rich, multifaceted symbol that permeates literature, art, and media. Through poetry, prose, visual art, theatre, film, music, and digital media, this question reveals the depth of human emotions and the importance of food in our lives.

By exploring the literary and artistic representations of "Did you eat?" we gain a deeper understanding of the cultural and emotional significance of this universal question. It is a testament to the enduring power of food as a means of connection, care, and expression.

As we continue our journey, we will examine how modern society views and practices the act of asking "Did you eat?" Join us in the next chapter as we explore the contemporary implications of this timeless inquiry in the context of technology, globalization, and changing social norms.

Chapter 7: Modern-Day Implications

Introduction

As we journey into the modern era, the question "Did you eat?" continues to hold significant weight, albeit in evolving contexts. This chapter explores how contemporary society views and practices the act of asking "Did you eat?" and examines the impact of technology, globalization, and changing social norms on this timeless inquiry.

Quote: "The only constant in life is change." - Heraclitus

Changing Dynamics: The Modern Family

The structure and dynamics of families have evolved significantly over the past few decades. Traditional roles are being redefined, and the question "Did you eat?" reflects these changes.

Research: According to a Pew Research Center study, the number of dual-income households has increased dramatically, with both parents working full-time in nearly half of all U.S. families. This shift has altered traditional domestic responsibilities, including meal preparation.

Quote: "The strongest families are those where both partners share the responsibilities and joys of caregiving." - Unknown

Case Study: In many modern families, meal preparation and caregiving duties are shared more equitably between partners. Fathers are increasingly involved in cooking and caring for their children, challenging traditional gender roles. The question "Did you eat?" is now asked by both parents, reflecting a more balanced approach to family care.

Fun Fact: In Sweden, government policies promoting parental leave for fathers have significantly increased the involvement of men in caregiving roles. Swedish fathers are now more likely to take an active role in feeding and caring for their children.

The Role of Technology

Technology has transformed the way we communicate, and the question "Did you eat?" has adapted to these changes. Digital communication tools, social media, and mobile apps have created new ways to connect and share meals, even when physically apart.

Example: Video calling apps like Zoom and Skype have made it possible for families to share meals virtually. During the COVID-19 pandemic, many families and friends turned to virtual dinners to stay connected and maintain social bonds.

Quote: "Technology is best when it brings people together." - Matt Mullenweg

Case Study: During the pandemic, a family in New York used Zoom to have weekly virtual dinners with their relatives

in California. They would cook the same meal and eat together, asking each other "Did you eat?" as they shared stories and laughter across the digital divide. This practice helped them maintain a sense of normalcy and closeness despite the physical distance.

Fun Fact: The hashtag #VirtualDinnerParty gained popularity on social media during the pandemic, with thousands of posts showcasing families and friends connecting over meals via video calls.

Research: A study by the Journal of Social and Personal Relationships found that virtual meals can help maintain emotional closeness and support among family members and friends, even when they are unable to meet in person.

Globalization and Fusion Cultures

Globalization has brought diverse cultures closer together, leading to the fusion of culinary traditions and the sharing of food-related practices. The question "Did you eat?" reflects this cultural exchange and the blending of different food customs.

Example: In multicultural cities like New York, London, and Sydney, it is common to see fusion cuisine that combines elements from various culinary traditions. Asking "Did you eat?" in these settings can lead to conversations about new and exciting food experiences.

Quote: "Food is our common ground, a universal experience." - James Beard

Case Study: A restaurant in London serves a menu that blends Indian and British cuisine, offering dishes like tikka masala shepherd's pie. The restaurant's patrons often share stories about their culinary adventures and ask each other "Did you eat?" to exchange recommendations and experiences.

Fun Fact: The popularity of food trucks in cities worldwide has introduced people to a variety of fusion cuisines, from Korean-Mexican tacos to Indian-Chinese noodles, reflecting the global culinary melting pot.

Research: A report by the World Tourism Organization highlights that food tourism has become a major trend, with travelers seeking out unique culinary experiences and local flavors. The question "Did you eat?" often serves as an icebreaker and a way to connect with locals and learn about their culture through food.

Social Media and the Digital Food Culture

Social media has revolutionized the way we share and experience food. Platforms like Instagram, Facebook, and TikTok have made it easy to share photos, recipes, and food experiences with a global audience. The question "Did you eat?" has found a new home in the digital food culture.

Example: Food influencers and bloggers often ask their followers "Did you eat?" to engage with their audience and share meal ideas. These platforms have created virtual communities centered around food, where people can connect and share their culinary passions.

Quote: "People who love to eat are always the best people." - Julia Child

Fun Fact: The hashtag #Foodie has over 250 million posts on Instagram, showcasing the global fascination with food and the joy of sharing culinary experiences.

Case Study: A food blogger in Australia started a weekly live cooking show on Instagram during the pandemic. She would ask her followers "Did you eat?" at the beginning of each session, encouraging them to cook along with her and share their results. This interactive approach helped build a strong sense of community among her followers.

Research: A study published in the journal "Appetite" found that social media can influence eating habits and food choices, as people are often inspired by the meals and recipes shared by their peers and favorite influencers.

The Impact of Modern Lifestyles

Modern lifestyles, characterized by busy schedules and fast-paced living, have influenced how we ask and respond to the question "Did you eat?" Convenience foods, meal delivery services, and dining out have become integral parts of contemporary life.

Example: Meal delivery apps like Uber Eats, DoorDash, and Deliveroo have made it easier for people to access a variety of foods without the need for cooking. The question "Did you eat?" is now often followed by recommendations for the best local eateries or the latest trending dishes on these apps.

Quote: "In the fast-paced world we live in, sharing a meal together is a revolutionary act." - Unknown

Case Study: A group of coworkers in New York City uses a meal delivery app to order lunch together every Friday. They ask each other "Did you eat?" as they discuss their favorite dishes and explore new cuisines, fostering camaraderie and connection in the workplace.

Fun Fact: The rise of "ghost kitchens" – commercial kitchens that prepare food solely for delivery – has transformed the restaurant industry, offering a wider range of options for busy individuals and families.

Research: According to a report by Statista, the global online food delivery market is expected to reach $154.34 billion by 2023, reflecting the growing demand for convenient meal options in modern society.

Balancing Tradition and Modernity

While modern lifestyles and technological advancements have transformed the way we ask and answer "Did you eat?", many people still strive to balance these changes with traditional practices. Family meals, cultural rituals, and communal dining remain important aspects of maintaining connections and preserving cultural heritage.

Example: In Italy, despite the busy lives of modern families, Sunday lunch remains a cherished tradition. Families come together to share a leisurely meal, asking "Hai mangiato?" as they catch up and enjoy each other's company.

Quote: "Tradition is not the worship of ashes, but the preservation of fire." - Gustav Mahler

Case Study: A family in Japan, despite their hectic schedules, makes it a point to have dinner together at least three times a week. They ask each other " (Gohan o tabemashita ka?) as they share stories and maintain their cultural practice of communal dining.

Fun Fact: In many cultures, special occasions and holidays are marked by traditional meals that bring families and communities together, reinforcing the importance of food in cultural preservation.

Research: A study published in the "Journal of Family Psychology" found that regular family meals are associated with better communication, stronger family bonds, and improved mental health outcomes for both children and adults.

Conclusion: The Enduring Significance of "Did You Eat?"

The question "Did you eat?" remains a powerful expression of care and connection in the modern world. As we navigate the complexities of contemporary life, this simple inquiry continues to bridge gaps, foster relationships, and maintain cultural traditions. Whether through digital communication, globalization, or modern lifestyles, the act of asking "Did you eat?" reflects our enduring need to connect, nurture, and support one another.

As we conclude our exploration of this universal question, we are reminded of its profound significance in human experience. The question "Did you eat?" is more than a concern for physical nourishment; it is a testament to the power of food as a means of expressing love, care, and community.

In the next chapter, we will explore the future implications of this question and how it will continue to shape our interactions and relationships in an ever-changing world. Join us as we delve into the possibilities and challenges that lie ahead for the simple yet profound inquiry, "Did you eat?"

Chapter 8: Future Implications

Introduction

As we look towards the future, the question "Did you eat?" will continue to evolve and adapt to the changing dynamics of society. This chapter explores the potential future implications of this simple yet profound inquiry, considering advancements in technology, shifts in societal norms, and the ongoing importance of food in fostering human connections. We will delve into the possibilities and challenges that lie ahead for this timeless question and examine how it will continue to shape our interactions and relationships.

Quote: "The future belongs to those who believe in the beauty of their dreams." - Eleanor Roosevelt

Technology and Innovation: The Next Frontier

Advancements in technology will play a significant role in shaping how we ask and respond to "Did you eat?" As we continue to integrate technology into our daily lives, new tools and platforms will emerge that facilitate and transform our culinary experiences and social interactions.

Smart Kitchens and IoT

The rise of smart kitchens and the Internet of Things (IoT) will revolutionize how we prepare and consume food. Smart appliances, connected devices, and AI-powered assistants will streamline meal planning, cooking, and nutrition tracking, making it easier to ensure that we and our loved ones are well-fed.

Example: Imagine a smart refrigerator that monitors the freshness of your food, suggests recipes based on available ingredients, and notifies you when it's time to eat. Integrated with your smartphone, it could send a message to your family group chat: "Dinner is ready! Did you eat?"

Quote: "The kitchen of the future will be as much about connectivity as it is about cooking." - FoodTech Magazine

Fun Fact: Companies like Samsung and LG are already developing smart refrigerators equipped with touchscreens, cameras, and AI capabilities that offer personalized meal recommendations and track expiration dates.

Virtual Reality Dining

Virtual reality (VR) technology has the potential to transform the way we experience food and social interactions. VR dining experiences could allow people to share meals in immersive virtual environments, bridging physical distances and creating new opportunities for connection.

Example: A family scattered across different continents could gather in a virtual dining room, where they can see, hear, and interact with each other as if they were in the same place. They could share a meal, ask "Did you eat?" and enjoy each other's company in a fully immersive setting.

Quote: "Virtual reality will change the way we socialize, creating new dimensions for human interaction." - Tech Innovator

Fun Fact: VR dining experiences are already being explored by companies like Project Nourished, which aims to create immersive culinary adventures that engage all the senses.

Personalized Nutrition and AI

Artificial intelligence (AI) and machine learning will enable personalized nutrition plans tailored to individual needs and preferences. These technologies will provide real-time insights into our dietary habits, ensuring that we receive the right nutrients and maintain a healthy lifestyle.

Example: An AI-powered app could analyze your eating habits, health data, and preferences to create customized meal plans. It could send reminders and updates to your loved ones, letting them know that you are eating well and asking, "Did you eat your recommended meal for today?"

Quote: "The future of food is about personalization and precision."
- Nutrition Expert

Research: A study published in "Nature Medicine" found that AI-driven personalized nutrition plans can significantly improve dietary adherence and health outcomes, highlighting the potential of technology to support healthier eating habits.

Societal Shifts: Evolving Norms and Practices

As societal norms and practices continue to evolve, the question "Did you eat?" will reflect these changes. From shifting gender roles to changing family structures, this inquiry will adapt to new contexts and meanings.

Gender Equality and Shared Responsibilities

The movement towards gender equality will continue to influence how domestic responsibilities, including meal preparation and caregiving, are shared. The question "Did you eat?" will become a more inclusive expression of care, asked by all family members regardless of gender.

Example: In a household where both partners work and share domestic duties equally, asking "Did you eat?" will reflect a balanced approach to caregiving and nurturing, demonstrating mutual concern and support.

Quote: "True equality is when both partners take equal responsibility for the well-being of their family." - Gender Equality Advocate

Research: According to a report by the World Economic Forum, greater gender equality in domestic responsibilities leads to more balanced relationships, improved mental health, and better family dynamics.

Changing Family Structures

The definition of family is becoming more diverse and inclusive, encompassing a wide range of structures beyond the traditional nuclear family. The question "Did you eat?" will be asked in various family configurations, reflecting the evolving nature of familial relationships.

Example: In multigenerational households, single-parent families, and chosen families, the act of asking "Did you eat?" will continue to signify care and connection, adapting to the unique dynamics of each family type.

Quote: "Family is not defined by our genes, but by the bonds we form and the care we show each other." - Family Therapist

Fun Fact: According to the Pew Research Center, the number of multigenerational households in the U.S. has increased significantly, reflecting changing economic and social trends.

Globalization and Cultural Exchange

Globalization will further enhance the cultural exchange of culinary traditions and practices. The question "Did you eat?" will reflect this diversity, incorporating elements from different cultures and fostering a greater appreciation for global cuisine.

Fusion Cuisine and Culinary Exploration

The blending of culinary traditions will continue to create new and exciting food experiences. The question "Did you eat?" will invite conversations about diverse flavors and fusion dishes, encouraging culinary exploration and cultural exchange.

Example: In a multicultural city, friends from different cultural backgrounds could share a meal that combines elements of their respective cuisines. Asking "Did you eat?" becomes an opportunity to learn about each other's culinary traditions and preferences.

Quote: "Food is a passport to understanding and appreciating the richness of diverse cultures." - Culinary Historian

Fun Fact: The global popularity of fusion cuisine has led to the creation of unique dishes like sushi burritos, kimchi tacos, and butter chicken poutine, reflecting the blending of culinary influences.

Food Diplomacy and Cultural Understanding

Food can serve as a powerful tool for diplomacy and cultural understanding. The question "Did you eat?" will play a role in fostering cross-cultural connections and promoting peace through shared culinary experiences.

Example: International culinary exchange programs, where chefs and food enthusiasts from different countries share their culinary traditions, can help build bridges between cultures. Asking "Did you eat?" in these contexts can lead to meaningful conversations and a deeper appreciation for global diversity.

Quote: "Breaking bread together is one of the oldest and most enduring forms of diplomacy." - Cultural Ambassador

Research: A study published in the "Journal of Peace Research" found that cultural exchange programs, including culinary exchanges, contribute to improved diplomatic relations and mutual understanding between countries.

Challenges and Opportunities

While the future holds exciting possibilities for the question "Did you eat?" there are also challenges to consider. Addressing issues such as food security, sustainability, and the digital divide will be crucial in ensuring that this inquiry remains a meaningful expression of care.

Food Security and Sustainability

As the global population continues to grow, ensuring food security and sustainability will be paramount. The question "Did you eat?" will take on new significance in the context of efforts to provide nutritious and sustainable food for all.

Example: Innovative solutions like vertical farming, lab-grown meat, and sustainable agriculture practices will play a crucial role in addressing food security. Asking "Did you eat?" will reflect a commitment to providing healthy and sustainable food for future generations.

Quote: "The future of food lies in our ability to innovate and create sustainable solutions for a growing world." - Environmental Scientist

Research: According to the Food and Agriculture Organization (FAO), sustainable agriculture practices are essential for achieving food security and ensuring that everyone has access to safe and nutritious food.

The Digital Divide

While technology offers many opportunities, the digital divide remains a significant challenge. Ensuring that everyone has access to the benefits of technological advancements in food and nutrition will be critical in making the question "Did you eat?" inclusive and equitable.

Example: Efforts to bridge the digital divide, such as providing internet access and digital literacy training in underserved communities, will help ensure that everyone can benefit from advancements in food technology and virtual connections.

Quote: "Bridging the digital divide is essential for creating a more inclusive and equitable future." - Technology Advocate

Research: A report by the International Telecommunication Union (ITU) highlights the importance of addressing the digital divide to ensure that all individuals can participate in and benefit from the digital economy.

Conclusion: The Timeless Inquiry in a Changing World

As we look towards the future, the question "Did you eat?" will continue to adapt and evolve, reflecting the changing dynamics of our society. Whether through technological innovations, shifting societal norms, or cultural exchanges, this simple inquiry will remain a powerful expression of care, connection, and community.

By exploring the future implications of "Did you eat?" we gain insight into the enduring significance of this question and the opportunities and challenges that lie ahead. As we navigate the complexities of the modern world, let us remember the timeless power of this inquiry to bring people together, nurture relationships, and foster a sense of belonging.

In the final chapter, we will reflect on the journey we have taken through the cultural, emotional, psychological, and societal dimensions of the question "Did you eat?" and consider the lessons we can carry forward into the future. Join us as we conclude our exploration of this universal expression of care and connection.

Chapter 9: Reflections and Lessons for the Future

Introduction

As we conclude our exploration of the question "Did you eat?" we look back at the diverse cultural, emotional, psychological, and societal dimensions we have uncovered. This final chapter reflects on the insights gained and the lessons learned from our journey. We will consider how this simple yet profound inquiry can continue to enrich our lives and foster deeper connections in an ever-changing world.

Quote: "The best journeys answer questions that in the beginning, you didn't even think to ask." - Jeff Johnson

The Universality of "Did You Eat?"

The question "Did you eat?" is a universal expression that transcends cultural and linguistic boundaries. It is a testament to the shared human experience of caring for one another and ensuring the well-being of those we love.

Key Insight: Regardless of where we come from, the act of asking "Did you eat?" reflects our innate desire to connect and nurture. This inquiry serves as a bridge that unites us across different cultures and backgrounds, highlighting the common threads that bind us together as a global community.

Quote: "There is no love sincerer than the love of food." - George Bernard Shaw

The Emotional Depth of a Simple Question

Throughout our journey, we have seen how the question "Did you eat?" carries profound emotional significance. It is a way of expressing love, care, and concern for others, providing comfort and reassurance in times of need.

Key Insight: The emotional impact of asking "Did you eat?" goes beyond the physical act of eating. It is an expression of empathy and compassion, a way to show that we are thinking of and caring for the well-being of others.

Example: In times of crisis or hardship, the question "Did you eat?" can offer solace and support, reminding individuals that they are not alone and that someone cares for their well-being.

Quote: "Food is symbolic of love when words are inadequate." - Alan D. Wolfelt

Cultural Significance and Traditions

The cultural significance of "Did you eat?" varies across different societies, reflecting unique traditions, values, and social norms. This question is deeply embedded in the fabric of cultural practices, from communal meals to festive celebrations.

Key Insight: Understanding the cultural context of "Did you eat?" allows us to appreciate the diverse ways in which food and caregiving are intertwined in different societies. It highlights the importance of respecting and valuing cultural traditions while embracing the richness of global diversity.

Example: In many cultures, communal dining is a central aspect of social life, where the question "Did you eat?" fosters a sense of belonging and togetherness.

Quote: "Food is our common ground, a universal experience." - James Beard

Psychological Perspectives: Nurturing and Bonding

From a psychological perspective, the question "Did you eat?" plays a crucial role in nurturing and bonding. It strengthens relationships and fosters a sense of security and trust.

Key Insight: The act of asking "Did you eat?" reinforces emotional bonds and creates a foundation for secure attachment, particularly in the context of family and caregiving. It is a powerful tool for building and maintaining relationships.

Example: Parents asking their children "Did you eat?" not only ensure their physical nourishment but also reinforce their emotional connection and support.

Quote: "To a mother, a child is like the beam of moonlight." - Chinese Proverb

Societal Implications: Gender Roles and Equality

Our exploration of the sociological perspectives behind "Did you eat?" revealed the impact of gender roles and societal expectations. While traditionally associated with women's caregiving roles, this question is increasingly becoming a shared responsibility in modern families.

Key Insight: Challenging traditional gender roles and promoting equality in caregiving responsibilities can lead to more balanced and fulfilling relationships. The question "Did you eat?" serves as a reflection of evolving societal norms and the progress towards greater gender equality.

Example: In dual-income households, both partners sharing the responsibility of meal preparation and asking "Did you eat?" demonstrates a commitment to mutual care and support.

Quote: "True equality is when both partners take equal responsibility for the well-being of their family." - Gender Equality Advocate

Modern and Future Implications

Looking ahead, the question "Did you eat?" will continue to evolve in response to technological advancements, changing family structures, and global cultural exchanges. It will remain a vital expression of care and connection in an increasingly interconnected world.

Key Insight: Embracing technological innovations and cultural diversity can enhance the ways we ask and respond to "Did you eat?" while preserving the core values of empathy, care, and community.

Example: Virtual reality dining experiences, personalized nutrition plans, and the blending of culinary traditions will create new opportunities for connection and understanding.

Quote: "The future belongs to those who believe in the beauty of their dreams." - Eleanor Roosevelt

Lessons for the Future

As we reflect on our journey, several key lessons emerge that can guide us in the future:

Embrace Diversity: Appreciate and respect the diverse cultural practices and traditions associated with food and caregiving. Recognize the richness that cultural exchange brings to our understanding of "Did you eat?"

Foster Empathy: Continue to use the question "Did you eat?" as a means of expressing empathy and concern for others. Let it be a reminder of the importance of nurturing and supporting those around us.

Promote Equality: Advocate for gender equality in caregiving responsibilities and challenge traditional roles. Encourage shared responsibilities in meal preparation and caregiving within families.

Leverage Technology: Embrace technological advancements that enhance our ability to connect and care for one another. Use technology to bridge physical distances and create new opportunities for shared culinary experiences.

Preserve Traditions: While adapting to modern changes, strive to preserve and honor traditional practices that foster a sense of community and belonging. Balance innovation with cultural heritage.

Conclusion: The Enduring Power of "Did You Eat?"

The question "Did you eat?" is a timeless and universal expression of care, love, and connection. It transcends cultural, linguistic, and societal boundaries, reflecting our shared human experience. As we move forward, let us carry the lessons we have learned from this journey and continue to use this simple yet profound inquiry to nurture our relationships and build a more connected and compassionate world.

Final Quote: "The journey of a thousand miles begins with one step." - Lao Tzu

As we conclude this book, may the question "Did you eat?" continue to remind us of the importance of caring for one another, fostering connections, and creating a world where everyone feels valued and supported. Thank you for joining us on this exploration of the cultural, emotional, and societal significance of this timeless inquiry. May your future interactions be filled with empathy, understanding, and the warmth of shared meals.